How To Write Poetry
For Beginners in 24 Hours or Less

By: Stephen Jones

AF228063

Introduction

I want to thank you and congratulate you for downloading the book, *"How To Write Poetry For Beginners in 24 Hours or Less"*.

This book contains proven steps and strategies on how to write poems as a beginners in less than 24 hours. You do not need to have years of experience in composing poetry in other to compose a great poetry.

With steps by step process on how to achieve this, I have decided to simply just to ensure that anyone can actually read this book and understand it. So keep reading and welcome to the world of poetry.

Thanks again for downloading this book, I hope you enjoy it!

Syllble Writer Bio

Vladimir Edouard

Vladimir Edouard, writer, and filmmaker. He enjoys spending time with his family and getting lost in the ancient solitude of Florida's nature life.

Elena Novak

Elena Novak is in her second year of pursuing a master's degree in International Development at Clark University in Worcester, Massachusetts. She received her bachelor's degree in Creative Writing in 2014, then spent two years teaching English in Spain. She has experience as a published journalist and poet, but this is her first foray into fiction writing.

Sam Luebbers

Currently working as a Peace Corps volunteer in Ukraine, Sam received degrees in International Affairs and Marketing from FSU, where he also discovered his love for writing, so long as it wasn't for school.

Sarah Palmer: Vignette 3

Sarah sat at the edge of her bed and listened. What she was hearing was internal, not external. Her racing thoughts were bent on something new and strange. She found herself lately with more energy than usual; she was restless and excited. A month ago, she felt directionless but now, she felt like she had a reason to get up in the morning. She knew the reason, but she was reluctant to admit it to herself. Elias had brought out parts of her she'd never realized were hidden. Still, there was something about Elias that didn't sit right with her. He'd disappear for hours or days at a time, then act like he was never gone. She wasn't sure she could trust him, but there was something about him that drew her to him, like a kindred spirit. He seemed internally conflicted, as she was. What was it that tore him apart? She wondered.

She got up from her bed and turned on her computer. She clicked on the Bookmarks tab and pulled up a folder she hadn't touched in a long time: FBI. Signing onto the website, she began a job application.

Elias abandoned the effort and waited until the water was no longer brown before he splashed some of it against his face. In another new apartment, living another new life, these words were his only truth, the single thread he hoped to follow one day to escape the labyrinth of his own mind. He hated them, but they were his routine. Every morning he was honest, every day he lived innumerable lies and every night, he returned to his only confidant, honest once more. Yet today, even this practice, felt untrue. The eyes in the mirror had betrayed a single instance of doubt.

"Sarah."

And the thought of losing his mind excited him.

Elias: Vignette 1

He pulled at the broken chain he had struggled to find, and the yellow bulb flickered, held its breath, and then burst into a brilliant, harsh light, accentuating all that was imperfect in the room. The porcelain of the toilet in a losing battle to the incessant advance of rust, the black mold, spawned from a bathtub stained yellow, creeping through the grout, follicles of hair and skin, cast off by those who had themselves been forgotten, littered throughout, and a cloudy mirror, which now held the face of the apartment's most recent tenant.

"My name is Elias."

"I am not American."

"I do not remember the face of my father, I cannot recall the arms of my mother."

"I have never met myself, doing so would risk everything"

"I live at the behest of a man I have never met, for a purpose I am ignorant of. But it is the only way I can continue to live."

"I dream of another life."

The pace of his words slowed; a fly began its long and slow death against the warm, electric, glass.

"I have never loved. I do not love my country. I do not love my life. I do not love," he paused, briefly, as if trying to recall the rest, "another. I do not love myself."

The face in the mirror was unmoved.

© Copyright 2019 by Stephen Jones - All rights reserved.

This document is geared towards providing reliable information based on studies and research in regards to the topic and issue covered. Any information or advice given within this book may change overtime. The author will not be held reliable for any action or results that the reader may decide to take upon the given information. The publication is sold with the idea that the publisher is not required to render accounting, officially permitted, or otherwise, qualified services. If advice is necessary, legal or professional, a practiced individual in the profession should be ordered.

- From a Declaration of Principles which was accepted and approved equally by a Committee of the American Bar Association and a Committee of Publishers and Associations.

In no way is it legal to reproduce, duplicate, or transmit any part of this document in either electronic means or in printed format. Recording of this publication is strictly prohibited and any storage of this document is not allowed unless with written permission from the publisher. All rights reserved.

The information provided herein is stated to be truthful and consistent, in that any liability, in terms of inattention or otherwise, by any usage or abuse of any policies, processes, or directions contained within is the solitary and utter responsibility of the recipient reader. Under no circumstances will any legal responsibility or blame be held against the publisher for any reparation, damages, or monetary loss due to the information herein, either directly or indirectly.

Respective authors own all copyrights not held by the publisher.

The information herein is offered for informational purposes solely, and is universal as so. The presentation of the information is without contract or any type of guarantee assurance.

The trademarks that are used are without any consent, and the publication of the trademark is without permission or backing by the trademark owner. All trademarks and brands within this book are for clarifying purposes only and are the owned by the owners themselves, not affiliated with this document.

Chapter 1

Introduction

Poetry is a part of literature that I deem very interesting. As a beginner who wants to learn how to create poetry, not many things are required of you. One essential thing I advise anyone who wants to start creating poetry is that they should always allow their heart to have its place in poetry. Poetry has a lot of emotions attached to it. So to be an outstanding poet, you need to be a kind of person that can connect with emotions very easily. Be it the sad, happy, loving, angry, or whatever kind of emotion you can think of.

What is Poetry? Poetry is a part of literature that involves an imaginative awareness, where a specific emotion or an experience is passed across with a language that is arranged for its meaning, rhythm or sound. As a beginner who is just getting into the world of poetry, I must confess that the whole idea might be really overwhelming at first. Because putting down feelings and emotions on paper is not so easy. How can you really write down a feeling that there is hardly a word that describes it? Or how do you write down a feeling that can only be expressed?

Whatever the case may be, one thing still remains the same, and that is that you should bear in mind is that no famous poet became famous overnight. But through dedication, practice and experience you would realize that poetry is easy as it is also a very significant way to pass across the feeling of love. So, before we go forward as to how to create poetry as a beginner, there are some few things that you need to be aware of.

Introduction to Poetry as a Beginner

Poetry, as I said earlier, is a really great way to pass across an emotion feeling with words. There are lots of things that are involved in poetry you need to know before you can boldly start creating really great poetry. And I sincerely hope that this comprehensive list I have complied would be of help to your poetry adventure.

• KNOW YOUR GOAL

First and foremost I would like for us to start with the goal of your poem. There are so many different types of poetry out there. So out of this many different types of poems, you have to choose which one or combination truly passes your type of message.

If you do not know where you are going, there is entirely no way you are going to get there. So you have to sit down and understand why you are even going into creating poetry in the first place. So that you can set the right goal in mind. Ones your goal is set correctly, then you can be sure that it would help you get the right inspiration.

• AVOID CLICHÉ

Cliché is another thing you need to know as a poet and avoid them. Why should I avoid cliché as a poet? Well because you are creating poetry and poetry is meant to carry so many emotions attached to it. Clichés are words that have been used too many times that it does not have any more effect on people. For example busy as a very, or tired as a dog, are examples of clichés.

People see clichéd words as fake, and when you use such in your poetry, it would seem as though your poetry is fake. And as a beginner when people start criticizing your poetry, it can easily discourage you from your dream. So avoid clichés

• AVOID SENTIMENTALITY

As a beginner, you should avoid using sentimental words when creating poetry. When people notice that your poetry is shifting from love and passionate poem to pity and self-centered poem, they will not take it seriously. Although making use of sentimental words are not all bad if you know how to use them.

As you advance with time, you would be become quite good and playing with words. And in no time you would notice that you make us of sentimental words without people even realizing it. The main problem with sentimentality that assumes beginner you should avoid is that it detracts from the literary quality of your work.

- ## USE IMAGES

So basically when you are creating poetry, it has to be able to stimulate your reader's sight, smell, touch, hearing, taste, and motion. You can achieve all this by capturing the image in your mind with words. When you write, do not just tell your readers about what you are trying to let them know, instead show them what you are trying to tell them with your words.

You need to be able to paint with your words. This is in fact not so easy at first, so do not get discouraged if you find it difficult at first. Just try to be as creative as you can with your words. Play around with your words and let your readers explore a whole new world of emotion with your words.

- ## USE SIMILES AND METAPHORS

You can also create really great poetry with similes and metaphors. You should also note that it does not mean that when you use a smile or metaphor in your poetry, your poetry would automatically be great. Poetry is all about creativity.

To create really great poetry, you need to be able to use the simile and metaphor properly in your poetry. So to bring imagery and concrete words into your poetry use the smile and metaphor.

- ## AVOID ABSTRACT WORDS, RATHER USE CONCRETE WORDS

Use of concrete words is another vital point you need to take note of as a beginner. Concert words are used to describe the things that people can see and feel with their sense. When a poet makes use of a concrete word in the poem, readers can actually relate to the poem better since they can feel the words being used with their senses.

But abstract words, on the other hand, is a whole different ball game on its own. Abstract words describe feelings or the concept of a thing. As a beginner, you should avoid abstract words. Perhaps as you advance with time, you will be able to get your grasp on how to play around with abstract words. But for now, just stick to the use of concrete words.

- ## COMMUNICATE THE THEME

When wrong a poem as a beginner ensure that you communicate the theme of the image of the poem you have in your mind. All poetry has a particular theme, and as such yours would require one too. Basically, your theme is actually about your idea and your opinion.

The theme of a poem is not a subject or a title. Instead, it is a statement about the event. When you can adequately communicate the theme of your poem to your readers, it would enable them to understand the poem better.

- ## SUBVERT THE ORIGINAL

As a beginner, I would love to tell you that you do not need to be a unique or literary genius in other to create really great poetry. Actually, I say you can even create great poetry as a beginner under 24 hours. Poetry is mainly about seeing what other people see every day but in a new and different way.

So long you are able to take an original place, object, idea or person and come up with a new redefined perspective about it and you can put it down in words, you a great poet. Being a great poet is all about reach the depth of inside you and bringing out a part of you that is new, and interesting.

• RHYTHM OF YOUR POEM

Another point to consider as a beginner poet is the rhythm of your poem. Rhythm is basically all about the amount of stress you place on a word. When you add rhythm to your poem, it makes it pleasing to the ears of your listeners, but be careful when you use rhythm though.

When you make use of rhythm the wrong way, it can be really dangerous. Most especially when you choose a rhythm that makes your poem seem like a song rather than a poem. When you do not make use of rhythm the right way, it can actually reduce the quality of your poem.

• REVISE

Last but not least, when you are done with composing your poem, you need to revise it over and over again. The reason why you need to revise it is that you need to be sure of the usage of words you made use of.

A lot of times many beginners after drafting their poem they feel as though they are through with the poem. But in truth, it is just the beginning when you are through with drafting the poem. To ensure that the poem is completely done and free from errors as well as portraying the exact message you are trying to pass across then you need to revise the poem thoroughly.

Now that you know what to expect from poetry let us now further proceed with proven steps by step process that has worked for me, my family members and a lot of my colleagues in putting down a poem in less than 24hours as a beginner. I would still love to mention that poetry is not as hard as it may seem at first. It just requires a lot of concentration and emotions. So sit tight as we go down the road of poetry for beginners together.

Here's a recap of this chapter:

- Poetry is a part of literature
- You need to be able to connect with emotions in other to write a great poem
- Poems are one of the best ways to write down what is being felt deep down in our hearts
- Avoid things like cliché words, abstract words, and sentimentality when composing your poem
- When composing your poem use concentrate words, ensure you communicate your theme, make your words imaginative not descriptive.

Chapter 2

The Environment

As a beginner who wants to get into the world of poetry but does not know how to begin worries no more for this guide would coach you on how to be a great poet in less than 24 hours or less. In other to get the best inspiration ever for your poem you need to set up your environment first then decided the goal of your poem.

I would not advise you as a beginner to just jump into second-guessing about what to write down in your poem. You have actually to sit down and think deep. Try to reach out to the innermost you and get those high emotions down on paper. So before you, we move any further let me show you how to get your environment setup.

Setting up the Environment

Your environment where you want to stay and create poetry is very crucial to your progress. You cannot imagine staying in a noisy and loud environment and expect to get good inspiration. In chapter 1 I made mention that poetry require a lot of concentration. This is because you are trying to put down what is being felt into writing and still portray that same message of what is being felt to the readers.

Your environment is very crucial to your progress, so set up your environment in other to be able to get great inspirations. How do I set up my environment? There is no need to ponder this question in your heart because there are not too many details about setting up your environment for creating poetry that you do not already know.

To set up your environment for creating poetry, first of all, you want to ensure that you set up a place that is not easily accessible by people. You want to choose an environment that people would not just barge into. A place like your room can do the magic for you. You can also decide to set up your basement for this purpose. And if you are a kind of outdoor person that loves to connect with nature, you can decide to set up a place at your backyard.

Perhaps you have a garden in your backyard, and even if you do not have a garden where you can easily plant one there. A garden too can be of great help in making your mind think more great poems. So plant those flowers and water them, tend to your garden yourself and those times you send just tending to your garden can just spark up inspiration from deep down inside you.

When setting up your environment, there are some specific things that must be in place before you can boldly say that your environment is perfect for creating poetry.

• **FREE FROM DISTURBANCE**

Your environment most for be free from any form of unwanted disturbance. I am not saying that your environment must be completely quiet because you can actually have music playing at the background to hack up your inspiration. But the kind of disturbance I am talking about here is an unwanted disturbance that is not caused by you.

Take, for example, you are sitting in the sitting room of your house, trying to concentrate your mind into creating a beautiful poem, and you keep hearing the screams of your neighbors' children as they play joyfully. This screams can be a really great disturbance as they would keep taking your to mind off track anytime you try to focus.

That is why I suggested that you set up an environment like your garage. When you are in your garage sounds from outside might not even get in at all, and if at all they do get in, it is just very minimal. You might not even hear the sound from outside except that you pay close attention to it.

- ## **SPACIOUS AND ORGANIZED**

So another thing to consider is a spacious space for creating poetry. You may want to ensure that your environment is not too clumsy. At times during trying to get a particular inspiration, you may need to do a little bit of demonstration. And to do any form of demonstration you need a spacious environment.

Also, the environment needs not only be spacious but also organized. Organized in the sense that whatever it is that you may need is right at your grasp and fast. One thing you need to know about inspiration and creating poetry is that as fast as inspiration gets into your head, that is how fast it goes away. Expect you take your time and record the inspiration it might get lost for life, never to be recalled again.

So you need to ensure that your environment is organized at all times. Even after you are done with a section of brainstorming for inspiration and you want to take a few minutes to break, it is still required of you that you organize the environment before you leave.

- ## **COMFORTABLE**

Also, I would like to stress the fact that your environment needs to be as comfortable as it can get. With proper lighting that even though you use the window blinds or you decide to get some fresh inspiration at night, you would have a well-lit room to make use of.

Apart from the lighting of the environment for comfort, the environment should also be well aerated to ensure that you are not working under stress. I have come to understand that the more comfortable an environment is, the more you would be able to get really great inspiration.

Do you also know that the sit-in which you sit on can also contribute to your comfort when you are working? Well basically anything that makes you comfortable, and at the same time would not distract you, can be included in the environment.

Now that you have your environment all set and ready, what is next? What is next is to get you into the environment you set up and create some of the best poems the world has ever heard.

Here's a recap of this chapter:

- Set up your environment to ensure you are comfortable
- You get better inspiration when your environment is set up to your taste
- A spacious, well organized and free from disturbance is a kind of environment that you should compose your poem

Chapter 3

Know Your Goal

Another very vital thing that needs to be considered as a beginner who wants to create poems in 24 hours or less is to decide the goal of your poetry. In chapter 1, I made mention of what the goal of a poem is, now in this chapter let us discuss in details what the goal of a poem entails.

You basically cannot create poetry if you do not have a goal in mind. The goal of poetry is what in fact determines the genre of the poem you compose. The idea that a poem is based on is also decided by the goal of the poem.

When you want to create any poem, the first question that you ask yourself is what the goal of this poem is? This question seems pretty easy to answer, and it is also quite straightforward too. But it is, in fact, the most crucial aspect of any poem. If you cannot seem to get the goal of your poem right, you would notice that you would have conflicting ideas.

You need to know what the poem you want to compose should do. The type of people that would benefit from the poem and why you choose them is all important in ensuring that you are able to write a lovely poem at the end of the day. As I have previously said, you cannot compose a poem if you have not decided on the goal of the poem.

To know the goal of your poem, there are a few steps that need to be taken to ensure that your goals are correctly set. You need to ensure that you set this at the utmost importance in other to be able to create a really great poem.

The Goals

The goal of poetry is what determines the type of poem you are going to do at the end of the day. You cannot set the goal of your poem to lay an impact on soldiers at war and expect that same poem to have the same effect on toddlers in school. So setting the right goal as a beginner who wants to create a poem under 24 hours is as important as getting the right inspiration for the poem.

When your goals are correctly set, your poem would be great. To get the best of goals figured out for your poem in less than 24 hours, get into the environment you set up previously in chapter 1. Once you are in your environment, everything else would just seem to become mute, more like you begin to shut yourself from this world and become alive in some world where you create with your imaginations.

Then as soon as you feel relaxed and settle in the environment, focus your mind on figuring out the what goals you want to set for the poem you are trying to compose. The process of figuring out the goals of your poem should not take you too long actually. The goal of a poem is simple, yet complex at the same time.

You do not really need to crack your head with length lust of goals you want a poem to do. Actually the less the goals of your poem the higher the impact it would have. You may ask why is it like this? Well, it's because when you have fewer goals in mind you want your poem to do, you would be able to focus your mind more as to the things you want the poem to do.

So at that point agent, you are relaxed and ready to start creating poems, ask yourself this question, who am I writing this poem for? Why am I writing this poem? What do I want this poem to do? This three questions may seem shallow to you at first, but when you are able to answer these questions correctly, you would, in turn, realize that poem writing is even easier to you as a beginner than how hard people always say it is.

If you can figure out this question really quick, then you are making fast progress, but if not, do not feel down or like a very slow learner. Everything in life is a process, the fact that you are not getting it under the first 5 minutes, does not mean you would never get it in life. So just give it some little more thought, and you would be surprised at the fountain of inspiration that would spring forth out of you.

Figuring out the goal of your poem should not take you too long to figure out. Actually, you should spend approximately 1 hour or less trying to figure out the goal of your poetry. The truth is before you even decided to read this book, you already know what your goal is. Because it is when you already have a goal in mind that you would feel the urge to write a poem.

Perhaps you are reading this book because you want to write a poem for your lover and you need to do it under 24 hours or less. Or maybe you are trying to come up with a speech, and you feel a poem would do a lot of good in your speech, all these are typical examples of goals. So with your goals already figured out, we can now proceed to the next stage on how to poetry in 24 hours or less. Next on our agenda on writing a poem in 24 hours or less is how to focus our minds on getting inspirations for writing poems. So stay tuned.

Here's a recap of this chapter:

- Your goals are fundamental in ensuring that you compose a really great poem
- You cannot write such a poem without a poem, you would not get the right inspiration
- Do not feel discouraged if you don't already have a goal before you-you decided to compose something poem

Chapter 4

Inspiration

Now let us take our next step, and that is getting inspirations for writing poems. After having your environment set in less than 1 or 2 hours depending on what environment you want to make use of, and setting the right goals in your mind is less than 1 hour too. At this point, you must have spent just about 3 hours of your time in total. And now we shall get into the main problem here, and that is how to poetry.

If you are not well inspired, you will encounter a lot of roadblocks along your way to writing a great poem. A poem is all about writing down what emotionally touches your heart the most. There are different genres of poems, and each of them is inspired by different things.

You cannot expect what inspires a love poem to be still the same thing that inspires a poem about political corruption. So when you are trying to get inspiration to try to relate more with things that are connected to the genre of poem you are trying to compose. Poems should not be written for just writing sake, or written because you want the fame and applause, no, poems should be written only and when you get inspired by something.

The reason why a lot of people troop into poem writing and in no time they troop out is because they lack inspiration. As a beginner, I would advise that you do not write anything down until you have been appropriately inspired. When you are inspired by a thing, you become like a fountain of words, the words would flow out of you. It would even get to a point where perhaps after some few days, you come back to read your poem, you would be amazed at the choices of words you made use of, and you may even find it hard to believe that you were the one that wrote the poem.

A lot of great poets today would still tell you the same thing about writing a poem. Inspiration is the key to their success. So as a beginner, how do you get inspirations for writing poems? I would be giving you three significant ways you can easily connect to any genre of poem you want to write. These points have been used by many poets, and I can assure you that if you open up your mind to it, it would in no doubt inspire you as well. You may be surprised that you may even get more inspired than some of the greatest poet of all times.

How to Get Inspirations

As long as you can place yourself on the right track, inspirations would keep flowing like a stream of water in your mind. So with these three tips on how to get inspirations, you would be surprised at how you would start to write poetry like some professional. The truth is that a great poem is as a result of great inspiration. How you can connect with this also affect the way your inspiration flows.

The way you perceive things, your perception, your mindset towards things all contribute to the level of inspiration you get. That is why I previously said in chapter 1 that when you can connect with things emotionally, you would be a great poet. This is just because of the about of inspiration that you get when you are emotional. Emotions being the best out of anyone so you can have that at the back of your mind. Check out these tips on how to get inspirations:

- **LISTEN TO MUSIC**

Listening to music is one way of getting inspirations. Music is emotional, and when you are a music kind of person, it even makes the connection stronger. When you can connect with music very well, I would strongly advise that anytime you are trying to get some inspiration, have music playing in the background.

You do not necessarily need to do it as though you are throwing a house party. But rather have the music playing softly at the background with a low volume, at least low enough that you can hear and at the same time would not distract your mind from getting inspirations for the lines of your poem.

• FOCUS YOUR MIND

Another tip I would like to give you to enable you to get inspired is the power of the mind. You need to be able to focus your mind. Now when you sit down for a minute, or you stand whichever you prefer, try to focus your mind of things that are relating to your poem. If you are writing something, love poem thinks about love. Think about your experience with love, other people experience with love, you can even focus your mind on things you expect out of love.

A focused mind is just like a ticking time bomb ready to explode with inspiration. Focusing on the mind is one way a lot of great poet of today got to the level they are today. Nothing good they say comes easy, so do not expect focusing of the mind to come so easy. Our mind is just like a busy highway, tough to keep it in place. You may be focusing on a particular thing, and the next second your mind has wandered away. So ensure always to keep it in check.

• READING POEMS FROM GREAT POETS

Last, on the tips, I would like to give you on getting inspirations for writing poem is to read poems from other great poets. This is actually the best way to get inspirations. Because when you read the poems that are written by great poets, you would be able to focus your mind on the same things that gave those great poets inspiration. Great poets are experienced, and they know how to organize a poem best. So as a beginner, you can quickly tap into the world of poetry by merely reading the poems from great poets.

Here's a recap of this chapter:

- Inspirations are caused by what you focus your mind on

- There are various ways you can get inspirations depending on the genre of poem you want to write

- Do not write anything down when you have not gotten the right inspiration

Chapter 5

Compose the Poem

If you made it this far, I would first like to congratulate you as you are making quite a progress as a beginner. At this stage, you must have set up an environment, known the goal to your poem, gotten the right inspiration which should take you approximately 2 hours. So at this stage, we are talking about you spending an approximate of 5 hours.

The next stage we are about to move into now is the part I figure you have been waiting for since you started reading this book, which is how to compose the poem. So far so good, I have already briefed you on what to do in other to have a well-composed poem. But yet again I would still love to expound on them a little bit more. There are quite a few things that you need to do when you want to compose a really great poem.

A poem should not be composed in a rush so I would advise that you spend the most time here composing the lines of your poem. The lines of your poem should not be so long, try to keep them as short as you can. This is because it is a poem you are writing not a book. A line of 5-6 words would be just fine. And ensure that each of the lines is well organized portraying the right image you are trying to pass across to the reader.

Tips for Composing Poem as a Beginner

A poem is only beautiful when you can compose it well. To compose a great poem you have to take it slowly and step by step. Use the following tips to ensure that you stay on track when composing your lyrics.

- **AVOID CLICHÉ WORDS**

I have said this before, and I am saying it again, avoid cliché words when you are composing your lyrics. You want to ensure that your reader feels a connection with your poem.

And you do that you need to avoid cliché words because cliché word makes your work seem fake, not original, as though you are making up emotions. So try to keep your words as simple as you can, using simple terms and words that are real to people in this present century.

• MAKE USE OF IMAGE

This is another vital thing to remember when you are composing your poem. Do not just tell your readers about your inspirations its ideas, but rather show them with words, describe it Inna way that they can see it. You need to be able to use your words to paint an image for your reader to see. A poem goes beyond what is written on paper. A poem gets to the heart and soul of a man, so you need to be very creative with your words. Like a said before, a poem is meant to touch six senses in a person, that is the sight, hearing, smelling, touching, taste, and kinesiology meaning the sense of motions so direct your words to touch those senses.

• USE CONCRETE WORDS INSTEAD OF ABSTRACT WORDS

This is so another point that you need to consider as a beginner who wants to write a poem. If you want to be a great poet that everyone would love, then ensure your poems are written with concrete words instead of abstract words. Abstract words only refer to a concept or a feeling. When you make use of it in your poem, you are not really activating the six senses I mentioned your poem has to touch.

But on the other hand, when you make use of concrete words in composing your poem, your poem would be able to touch these senses effectively. This is because actual words describe things that are experienced by people, things that people use their senses to feel. When you use concrete worlds in your poem, it makes it very easy for people to connect with the poem and at the end, you would realize that you have become such a great poet in no time.

This tips I just outlined are just a few of the numerous tips that you can get about how to compose a poem. But I decided to give you these few ones because they are the most essential of them all. When you have these tips at the back of your mind, you would realize that composing someone poem would be a piece of cake.

Here's a recap of this chapter:

- Take your time while composing a poem

- There is no need for a rush when composing a poem

- Tips like avoiding cliché words and abstract words should be what your poem is keyed on

- Making use of concrete words and imaginative words should be what your poem is keyed on

Chapter 6

Revise

After you are done composing your poem which should take you quite some time, but I suggest you spend between 3-4 hours putting down your wordings composing the whole poetry. You should not also forget about the rhythm of the poem. Get a really nice rhythm for the poem and then to revise the entire poem to ensure that you are completely through with the poem.

The whole process of composing a poem is fascinating and thrilling, from setting up an environment to knowing the goals of the poem. It might get pretty challenging in the beginning just going through all those brainstorming times all for the sake of putting down some words. But at the end of it all, it is totally worth it. Also from knowing your goals to getting inspired can also be quite challenging as you may start getting some conflicting thoughts as to how to even get inspirations from your goals you have set.

I am pretty sure you found the hardest part to be converting your inspirations to a well-composed poem. And since you did not let that discourage you, here we are at the final stage of how to poetry. The final step to take after all has been said and done is to revise your poem. You may feel as though there is no need for revising it, but actually revising your poem at the end of the day is as important as any other stage you passed through while composing the poetry.

If after all the stress of trying to put the whole poem together, and you do not revise it is just like building a car and not testing it. You need to revise your poem in other to for you to be sure that your poem is good enough for your ears. Read the poem over and over again and ensure it is error free. No matter how good a writer you are, everyone is prone to making errors at one point or the other. While you are composing the poem, you might not realize the mistake, but when you are revising it, you will notice those errors you did not see in the first place.

For even a better way to revise your poem, put the poem away for a few hours and try to engage yourself in other things to distract your mind from the poem. Then on getting back revise through the poem again to ensure that everything is perfect. Then I'd everything is in perfect you can rest from the whole stress of composing poetry in 24 hours or less as a beginner.

But when you revise through your poem again, and you realize that there are some errors may be in your choice of words or the rhythm, then you need to edit it and revise it again quickly. It is just like a flow chart. If it passes the test, it proceeds to the next stage but it it does not, it goes back to the previous steps for corrective action and comes back for testing(revise) again.

So after revising for a couple of hours, and you can not seem to point your fingers on any error, then you can boldly say you have finally completed your poem in 24 hours or less as a beginner. So you see that anyone can actually write a poem all you need is just the right mindset and putting your mind to it.

Here's a recap of this chapter:

- Revise your poem in case of an error

- When you revise your poem, and it's error-free, then your poem is complete

- Revising your poetry is as vital as any other stage of composing a poetry

- You should put away your poem for some hours before you revise it again as this helps to ensure that your mind is fresh

- Revising your poem is like a flow chart when you revise your poem if it passes the test, it's all good, but if it does not, then it goes back to the previous steps and undergoes a corrective action then comes back for testing (revising)

Conclusion

Thank you again for downloading this book!

I hope this book was able to help you to help you figure out how to write a really love poem. I would also love to see some of the poems you were able to compose if you do not mind.

The next step is to explore more in the world of poem writing. As the popular saying does, experience is the best teacher. So keep writing more poems to be really good at writing poems.

Finally, if you enjoyed this book, then I'd like to ask you for a favor, would you be kind enough to leave a review for this book on Amazon? It'd be greatly appreciated!

Thank you and good luck!